Somewhere in the Middle of Love

by

Lisa A. Lipscomb

AuthorHouse™
1663 Liberty Drive, Suite 200
Bloomington, IN 47403
www.authorhouse.com
Phone: 1-800-839-8640

First published by AuthorHouse 9/25/2007

ISBN: 978-1-4343-1335-5 (sc)

Library of Congress Control Number: 2007903769

Printed in the United States of America
Bloomington, Indiana

This book is printed on acid-free paper.

authorHOUSE®

A journey of 1,000 miles begins with a single step

-Lao Tzu

People are unreasonable, illogical and self-centered;
Forgive them anyway.

If you are kind, people will accuse you of selfish, ulterior motives;
Be kind anyway.

If you are successful, you win some false friends and some true enemies;
Succeed anyway.

If you are honest and frank, people may cheat you;
Be honest and frank anyway.

What you spend years building, someone could destroy overnight;
Build anyway.

If you find serenity and happiness, they may be jealous;
Be happy anyway.

The good you do today, people will often forget tomorrow;
Do good anyway.

Give the world the best you have, and it may never be enough;
Give the world the best you've got anyway.

You see, in the final analysis, it is between you and God;
It was never between you and them anyway.

-Mother Teresa

My purpose for writing this book is to contribute to the pool of experiences, lessons and blessings that go hand in hand with loving relationships. Love reveals itself in many forms and fashions. It's always *right under our nose...* whether we find it in the beauty of a sunrise or the twinkling in a loved one's eyes, it's there. In the depths of our heart we feel it when we are *tuned in* and open to marinating in it's flow and basking in it's warmth and glow. Love has no beginning, nor an end. It is ever-present and eternal. So I find myself in the middle of love no matter which way I step or what lies before or behind me. The possibilities and opportunities for life, fulfillment, joy and love are endless for you and me. Let's dig deep and wide- expanding our lives to see, feel and be love...

All relationships happen for a reason, a season or a lifetime. Knowing that all relationships will not *last* and that "Happily Ever Now" may be the closest we get to "Happily Ever After" may be our reality. Suffice it to say, I accept that. There have been times when I didn't want the end of a relationship to come about... I know I am not alone. The hurt can be temporarily devastating. Let us not forget that we always have a choice to make in matters of love. We cannot control our circumstances, but we do control our reactions to them. We make the choice to fill a second, a minute, an hour, a day... or many with thoughts of Heaven or hell. After spending time being mad, angry, hurt... you name it- I've decided that forgiveness and healing are the routes that bring me a peaceful foundation. My poems are a reflection of that. I hope that after reading this collection, you find a peaceful and fulfilling place in your heart and continue to dwell there.

This book is dedicated to my parents, Sandra Lipscomb and the late Phillip M. Lipscomb Sr., whose love, support and foundation set the stage for the woman I am today. I thank my grandparents for their loving and nurturing attention. My siblings, Phillip and Stephanie who support all of my creative endeavors. My children, Jonathan, David and Kayla who are the motivation for most of what I do. It is my intent to love them to life. My family, friends, fellow teachers, poets, photographers and those who have always wanted to write a book... have a story to share and are on the path to doing so. Any and everyone who has ever had a dream and know it's part of the reason they are here. May you find and hold onto whatever inspiration you need to see it come true.

My prayer partner, friend, confidant and heart, Aaron R. Shell. Thank you for everything. I can't tell you how much my life has evolved since we've started spending so much of our time together, *being* with you is always a pleasure. I also appreciate the time you spent taking photos with me and your contribution to my work, the image used for the Relationship poem and the pictures of you and I that appear on the cover design, in addition, your calls of support, encouragement and constantly sharing so much great news. Simply put, our little *secret*, The Law of Attraction is a vital force which backs all of our efforts and brought us to the same space!

Renaissance Unity, all of the minister's who are there, and those who have come and gone. The choir, for dazzling our senses and energy with such great music. The members, whose kindred hearts and minds keep me lifted. My life has not been the same since I stepped into this sacred place.

Andi Kubaki, my graphic designer for assisting with my cover photo.

I would like to thank another photographer and encourager whose images capture both the attention and heart of many, Lee Bey. He contributed to this work with the photo that accompanies my poem " Touch."

Laretta Houston, thanks for your advice when I asked and encouragement always. Doris Judd, my other mother, you allow my heart a peaceful place to rest. Elnora Ford, your support throughout the years has been pivotal for me. Diane Arnold, you are a wonder to watch.

My cousin Caryl L. Polk and Aunt Carolyn O'Bryant have really encouraged me to move this project forward. Reminding me that the writing and sharing of these and the poems to come are part of my purpose for being here.

My Aunt Linda and cousin Tanya Lipscomb for your constant support.

My best friend on the planet and fellow poet, Rhonda Miller. You have been waiting over 15 years for me to write a book. I've always said I would… now consider it done!

The "Lunch Bunch," Donna Barnes, Leslee Hathaway, Odessa Nash, Terri Smith, Saleemah Tawwab- you were some of the first to hear my poems and share in the magic of my love for writing. In addition, all of the K.B. White Elementary School family.

Ms. Linda Edwards and the women who supported me during one of our Women's Circle meetings… you said I should publish and offered your ongoing support, thanks for everything! You were also the one who introduced me to my spiritual family and church home, Renaissance Unity, my life has been spiraling upward ever since.

I am eternally thankful to my Source, Creator and Gift Giver, God. My greatest blessing of all.

In the words of the apostle Paul…

Love is patient, love is kind.
It does not envy, it does not boast, it is not proud.
It is not rude, it is not self-seeking,
It is not easily angered, it keeps no record of wrongs.
Love does not delight in evil but rejoices in truth.
It always protects, always trusts, always hopes, always perseveres.
Love never fails…

I Corinthians 13: 4 - 6

Table of Contents
Part 1

Part 2

Part 3

Part 1

Of Spirit and Nature… as I choose to see things differently, the natural and ordinary becomes divine~

"When you are inspired by some great purpose, some extraordinary project, all your thoughts break their bounds… and you discover yourself to be a greater person by far than you ever dreamed yourself to be."

-Patanjali

With New Eyes

Dear Lord, sometimes I hide in a sleeping disguise
But today I pray to see with new eyes
New eyes to see the sun at dawn
New eyes as I stretch and stand and yawn
New eyes as I step out of bed, thanking You for the day which lies ahead
New Eyes as my eyes meet and greet Your children, passersby on the street

May the contact we make, include a smile, felt deep within ~connected by spirit
Our intent being to heal and mend
Let the meeting of our eyes and the feelings deep within add a light to the world, a flicker growing glow

May that light show us a path, get our energies to flow~ higher and lighter~ releasing~ and renewed
And the actions that follow be of good intent, reflecting more of You
And as my eyes see and my heart feels and my intentions turn toward You~
Please help me remember, embrace hope and surrender the burdens
that would make me feel blue

And as I wake with new vision and vigor, may the words I speak and the response they trigger be of love and light, that wakes us all and puts into flight…A dream world with a peaceful landscape, where babies and children and adults can escape…from the one with old eyes and closed eyes and dark hearts and destructive parts, led by ego and I could go on and on
But I can also stay focused on goodness, I **know** this

May we remain open to the changes needed within
May we be open, may we be free, may we spread peace and harmony
May there be space for joy and laughter, springboard for a cycle
which produces the desire to think again, and feel again,
and see with new eyes our world again

My Place

Somewhere in the middle of love
I experience total bliss
A visual wonderland, feeling sublime
Cradled by life's ever-present kiss

Feeling free and hopeful
Knowing all is well
Anticipating that only the best
Will be drawn up from my mind's wishing well

A place where time is eternal
With no beginning or end
Realizing this moment
Somewhere in the middle of love

Is the perfect time
And place
For my life to
Begin again

Regal

Lift me gently and I rise
Energetic whirlwind, weightless dance we comprise
Supporting one another's strength,
Blending our power, collective energy is intense
Beauty poised, balanced joy
Freedom, surrender, display so warm and tender

Sea of color floating through the air
You support me, as we behold His Presence~ everywhere

Gliding, sure, without worry or care
Knowing, being, dreaming, receiving…

That in this time, yes in this place
I am draped and enfolded in God's mercy and grace

I am joyous in this moment, alive, and free
Dancing with my love~ inspired by Thee

*Everyday brings a chance for you to draw in a breath,
kick off your shoes and dance*

-Oprah Winfrey

Dance With Me

Dancing is an art on the palate of our lives
Dancing is the entrance to our freedom, we up rise
Dancing is an expression of how we relate,
either gliding through
or marching to the songs of our life, so innate

Dance with me, my love, as the shackles fall free
allowing me to release past pain, dead energy

Dance with me as I unlock the chain of tension in my stride,
then loosen my shoulders, unbind my arms, the wall of fear inside

Dance with me as I let go of the shadows that do not exist,
And as I sweep the thoughts away that further inhibit my twist

Dance with me patiently and surely, as I learn to follow your lead,
Trusting your movement, your steps and the beat,
As we move together, time seemingly endless,
Adding laughter~ another dose of pleasure

Dance with me, though I'm still learning, we're learning,
yearning and turning
… and in time, burning up the floor

In the meantime, if I make a blunder, smile at me with your eyes,
and dance on…

Until we flow, blend together as one

"Just don't give up trying to do what you really want to do. Where there is love and inspriation, I don't think you can go wrong."

- Ella Fitzgerald

Sieve

How far can I take an idea
That passed through my thoughts
Last night as I was sleeping?

It stirred me awake
For goodness sake
As I woke, *realizing* that it was an idea worth keeping

So I grabbed a pencil
And paper to write it down
Brainstormed the possibilities, tossed them around
In my mind
Then added them to paper
Puzzling, piecing things together
Before losing my train of thought
To a foggy, escaping vapor

So as I sit
Thinking
Wondering what to write about
I'll unfold my arms, unblocking my thoughts
Then once again, words will begin to flow
As they always do
When ideas were meant
To work out

Flow

Moving forward
Surrendering
Letting go

Being lifted
Escaping
To a river below

Running to the edge
Dropping
Moving with the flow

Circulating always
Winding
On a course that offers me the potential to grow

What Really Matters

It is not the color of skin
That is the source of conflict
That stirs us from within

It is not the gender of an individual
That determines the amount of strength
That can be used to conquer or seemingly, set free

It is not the amount of money
That one possess or distributes
That determines self-worth

Nor is it the external beauty
That blossoms by day and fades
…in time
That validates genuine attractiveness

In matters of the heart
In matters of love
It is the spirit
The soul
The energy one brings
Carries
Delivers and shares
That makes the greatest difference

Do You Trust Me?

There are many times in life
That we have questions, without answers
Problems and are seeking solutions
Dilemmas that we want to get out of
Struggles that make us question
What we know, how things work
Realizing just how little control we have over life
And the many situations that we face
As we journey it's
Winding roads and oceans blue
One thing I know
No matter what
No matter how things happen or when
There is a promise
That keeps me
Supplies me with strength, hope
Energy, truth and all the trust I'll ever need, want and experience
God is
Wherever I am
Wherever my children are
Wherever my mother is
My father
My sister, brother
Friends, family are
Everywhere
Simultaneously
Forever and ever
Always has been
Always will be
Amen

When you come to the edge of all the light you know, and are about to step off into the darkness of the unknown, faith is knowing that one of two things will happen: There will be something solid to stand on, or you will be taught how to fly.

-Patrick Overton

Black-Eyed Susans

Golden yellow layers
Pause to say, "Hello"
As they quietly gather around
And watch each other grow

Greater Purpose

Of all the things that I may have
Both tangible and unseen
My heart, my body, my mind, my thoughts
My spirit, my soul, my dreams

My life serves a purpose
With lessons to learn and blessings to behold
Unwinding passages on a path with many directions
Choices unending, yet I have guidance and protection

Experiences and knowing
Yearning and growing
By way of an inner fire, central light
Intuition is a mystical presence, traveler's insight

Allowing me to be tuned in
To my life in this moment
The only time that truly is
I embrace and know it

Part 2

Family, Friends and a Community Spirit… the love and support we give ourselves and gather from others, nurtures and builds us up.

"Let us be grateful to people who make us happy, they are the charming gardeners who make our souls blossom."

-Marcel Proust

We Are Fruit from the Same Tree

As we gather together to celebrate the dream
Of our beloved Carrie Camille and all that she means…

Let us take this moment on which we reflect
And embrace peace and hope as our thoughts collect

We are one family, fruit from her seed
There is so much for us to share
There is much that we all need

We each serve a purpose, there are gifts that we all bring
And when blended together
Our lights grow brighter, casting out darker things

The running and hiding and secrets breed fear
The truth is a higher path
Raised above shadows of doubt… that will disappear

The answers we need are already here
We can embrace them together
They are forever near

As we take new steps together, stepping over our pain
We walk away from the past and surrender any hurt
That had been engrained

Our new path is love and the pebbles on the ground
Are support, praise and truth
Can we start our journey now? Are you ready to take part?
There is a power, a greater good and an eternal connection…

Where is your heart?

The love, life and dreams that Carrie helped to start
Carry on or stop with us

A legacy, our history
For generations our actions
Will tell of our intentions, wisdom we choose to impart

In case I've never told you or haven't said it lately
I love you, I believe in you
I'm glad that we are family

A Prayer for My Brother

I pray each day that as you wake
From a sleep that was refreshing
You start your day in a thankful way
Thanking God for all your blessings

And before you rise to get out of bed
Planting your feet on the floor
That you ask God for His guidance and strength
Before taking a step, making decisions
Walking out the front door

May you learn to embrace the love and blessings
That grow from a knowing in your heart
May you focus more on your greatest good
And surrender the things that are dark

An abundance of health
Taking care of yourself
Making decisions that bring peace, love, and joy
Accepting your role as a husband and father, a man~ no longer a boy

Life is lived from the inside out
The surroundings of the world around us
Reflect what's happening within
May you know your purpose and begin to work toward it
Can you imagine how sweet life would be then?

Letting go of what no longer serves you
Asking God to take the desires away
From the smoking and drinking, the choice to stop thinking
About things that cloud your vision , on any given day

I love you
I believe the best is yet to come
Stay focused, be prayerful
Set goals and just be
God is your source, He's got EVERYTHING you need
Don't ever forget it, believe it, receive it
I pray that your body, mind, and spirit are eternally freed

So my dear brother
What is it that you want?
Tell God, He's listening and will answer your prayers, indeed
His promises~ True, your life renewed, as you add water and light to His seeds

Windows

When I look into your eyes
It is love that I see
Traveling beyond time
Resting on the truth
Spreading out, reaching past endless possibilities

Visions of hope and faith…
Forgiveness draws us near
Embracing inner strength
Keeping our focus clear

My Sister, My Friend

It is you that has always said
That the dreams I have, and the talent I develop
And the love I share, the hope I create
The peace I pursue
Is mine, and yours, and the whole world's too

It is you that has always done
What you felt was right, what rang true in your soul
What made your heart swell with joy
The best that you could at any given moment
What you knew would empower yourself and others
To do and be, overflowing with passion
And tranquil radiant energy

It is you that has always been
A faithful friend
Whose word is gold
A woman of integrity, who stands boldly for truth
And that which uplifts
Bringing honor and promise, intangible gifts

It is I
That will always benefit
From our bond
Our being like-minded
Though we don't share DNA
The same last name
A mother, father
Or personality, tame

It is our creativity
Our compassion and consciousness
Beliefs and spirituality
That keep us together
Sisters in heart
And family forever

Thank You for Being My Friend

For the hours we've spent sharing…as we sat and broke bread
For the minutes we've spent caring…and making peace with our work bed
For the seconds we've spent talking…sharing thoughts, ideas and dreams

For the priceless moments witnessed…in memories that dance
For the exchange of our knowledge…in an effort to enhance
For the path that we all walk…our coming together was not by chance

For the lessons we've learned
For any support we've yearned
For the issues that touched us…making us all concerned

For the prayers and intercessions
For the love…
And heartfelt confessions

For the laughter …and any tears
For showing strength…and any fears
For the praise, compliments, smiles and cheers

For Odessa's passion and clarity
For Donna's service and sincerity
For our focused, sweet Saleemah
For Leslee being open and always giving
For Terri's glowing beauty and magnificent song
For Lisa's love of poetry
For our talents which bridge and balance us all

For the silent times
For the sharing of gifts
For the extra effort each Friday at lunch
For honoring our needs

For listening
For responding
For bonding
For being there
For knowing
For the time we've all spent growing
Thank you for being my friend

In union there is strength

-Aesop

Heaven's in you

-Kem Owens

Tribute to Our Choir

Did you hear the angels singing?
They are present~ in our midst
Did you hear the harmony
And music flowing from their lips?
Did you hear the praise and glory
As they sang and flowed, truly
Did you hear the testimony
Heartfelt knowing~ that it's all meant to be

Did you feel the power of their singing
Blessed gift from God alone
Did you feel the momentum growing
As they sang in unison, using both heart and tone
Did you feel the spirit quicken
In your heart and through your being?
Did you feel the truth in their words
As hands rose up... people stood...all in spirit, agreeing
Or did you chose to sit as tears fell from your eyes, endearing

Did you see the expressions on their faces
As they sang out for our God
Can you believe the glorious moments
As their gifts are shared out loud

Have you noticed that we've been invited to sing along and some dance
As Edward leads, the band plays, and Crystal narrates
Growing from seeds, all God's plants

Will you receive the opportunity to let your light grow brighter?
As we agree by being here,
We want our love to blossom
And spirits to fly higher

Will you believe that by being in this space of love today
That you are on a lighted path of holy ground
God assists you on your way

By rejoicing and receiving and believing, it's all true
That the gift of angels singing is only
The beginning of God's endless prosperity for you

Part 3

Recognizing Love in the Guise of a Relationship… relationships all serve a purpose. They show us who we are or are not, whether it is with ourselves or others… we can experience what it's like *to know* and *to be* love~

"You know when you're in love when you can't fall asleep because reality is finally better than your dreams."

-Dr. Seuss

Touch

Your touch
Penetrates my skin
And reaches deep
To the life that grows within

Relationship

A safe place for my heart to send and receive love,
A peaceful space for my spirit to be free...
Where I can be me and find acceptance,
Unconditionally

When my intentions are to share love, laughter,
And truth...where my life lessons are part of my proof,
That I have lived and grown, spent sometime alone...
Reflecting on what I can do, to help make my dreams come true

It is where my heart and mind move in agreement~
And I'm filled with peace and understanding,
With God leading me, many times I have seen it

When I am focused on goodness and my purpose
And am clear that my true calling is my service,
To do unto others as I would have them do me

Believing the vision we share is to be as joyous as we are free,
Listening to the Holy Spirit and moving in the direction that He
Has paved in order for our lives to stay together, beautifully

As we walk together and grow forever and our souls glow,
Radiating God's energy...

That's when I know that I have found a safe place
For my heart of hearts to reside, eternally

I Want To Be Touched By You

When I hear the sound of your voice, my attention gathers around your words and you capture my ear space

When I see the gaze of your eyes, my pupils rest easy as they wander into the gateways of your heart

When I smell the scent of your skin, polished with shea butter, earthed by tiny glands as you move about, my senses curl and I am awake

When I taste your lips as they envelope mine, I am aroused by our connection and embrace the high vibration of energy that we create in that moment

When I touch you, the lean firmness of your musculature, I remember that I want to be touched by you… the sound of your voice, the gaze of your eyes, the smell of your skin, the taste of your lips, the energy we create when we touch each other- physically, spiritually, intuitively

I know that life is fuller, more radiant and I breathe easier because I have been touched by you~

Taking Survey

There are times in our lives when we meet someone who
Adds a sparkle to our eyes and warm feelings to our heart
They extend the love we have to include
Intertwined laces of harmonious being

We sit, talk and laugh with another
Invest our time, thoughts, dreams and hopes for what can be and is

We know the potential
We subscribe to their magazine, their current life events, moments which
Leave us breathless and hopeful

We take a daily vacation
Creating images of our being together, both here and there…
On tropical islands, stretched out on sand
The beaches of our mind, with feelings grand

We want happily ever after
We want it now
A life we've always dreamed of, marinated in the energy of Wow

We want the best and believe it to be the person who sits across from *me*
A beautiful soul that means so much
We've happily crossed paths, we've learned, grown and touched

Then while in the midst of our magical flight
We start to look around, but there's only dim light
For the threads that once held us are loose
And unraveling
Yet we're still traveling

Trying to make it work
Straining and trying, bending and flying through the memories
That brought us no hurt

So I look at you and you glance at me
Searching for a glimmer of hope
We exercise our will to be
And together take another step
Then another with perhaps a brief pause to acknowledge that our journey
Could use some more pep

So we imagine that all is well
Simply because, we both believe that our willingness to overcome, will prevail

What lies behind us and what lies before us are tiny matters, compared to what lies within us.

-Ralph Waldo Emerson

Just Being

When I speak to you my heart feels free,
Relaxed, content and I can just be

You are a man who has threads of compassion, history,
Remembering and you're always ready to take action

Your spirituality is at the center of your being,
A man seeking God's approval
And you understand it's eternal meaning

You make me laugh and my heart sings
When I have thoughts of you
You add balance to my thinking and joy to my heart
Many moments that capture what's good and true

You are open and free, ambitious and can see
What's important and you're focused on it…

May you always be surrounded with people, places
And things that remind you of your greatness

You certainly bring out the best in me
Our meeting was at the right time and in the right place
…and your initial comment,
"I can see your heart through your eyes,"
Are words I will always embrace

Then you touched me, with a warm hug and a sure embrace
Your energy ran through me and now I look forward to being
In your space
May the time we spend together
Lift both our spirits to an even higher place

Unwinding

We came together
It was our destiny
We crossed paths for a reason
We've had our share of uplifting moments
We've had our share of some that got us down
All in less than one season

I said a prayer some months ago
And you've answered every one
I asked for you and my answer came true
You are my ray of sun

Did the Universe
Tap on your shoulder
When you turned to look at me?

Did you hear a whisper in your thoughts
That we'd come together
To be set free?

Did you see our future
And know that we'd connect
But later on
Though our feelings were still strong
We'd part ways
…could be a karmic debt

Did you taste the sweetness
In the kisses we shared
The depth of our feelings
Not to be compared

Did you imagine
That yesterday would come
No rain or clouds
Or feeling numb?

Just a touch of sorrow
Inspired by a change in mind
Of our being a couple
And the inevitable spinning
From the way things
unwind

Shades of Gray – Tales from a Hopeless Romantic

What do I do
When there is something
I want
That is not mine to have?

I think about it
Dream about it
Feel it
Walk around it
Smell it
Reach out for it
While pulling back
Retreating
Until I find myself engaged in another round
Getting myself all tangled up
Then unwinding again
Trying to define
My position
In a relationship
With my friend

Remembering

You opened the bottle
And poured me a glass
Of a bubbly, sweet, familiar wine

We sat back on the couch
I took a few sips
Shortly thereafter
Feeling, oh so fine

Then you opened
A box of chocolates
Pecan turtles…
Which you know are my favorite kind

And the light form the vanilla scented candles
Dancing on the ceiling
One of our relaxed moments in time

Then you looked at me
And I stared
Right back into your eyes
You inched in closer and
Whispered a bit, you initiated our
Hearts throbbing, imagination racing
Followed by quiet sighs

Our glasses now empty
So you refill mine
I'm feeling tipsy
Which is really no big surprise

Giggling, gazing
Talking, embracing
Feelings… a steady sublime

Lost in thought for a moment
Lost in time
Lost in memories, lost
Remembering what happened
When you were mine

You can encounter many defeats, but you must not be defeated
— Maya Angelou

Letting Go

Thoughts of you
Linger on
Despite the fact that you're now gone

I remember all the things you said
And the sweeping actions you made
The cradling of my thoughts...
My muse on uninspired days

The laughing and sharing
Of time, now past
A mutual choice
A journey we now take
Separately
Two paths on the same road

We reach out
But don't touch
Conscious of an incessant pain
Because it all still hurts
So much

Last Night

Last night as I lay sleeping
There was a knock from my heart to my head
Kind of quiet, but sure and deep

It whispered a thought into my head
After which I turned and tossed through the night in bed

So after a few hours, though it was still night,
I reached over, sat up and turned on the light

I opened my drawer and pulled out a list which was labeled, "Ideal Mate"
I read each adjective, noun and verb reviewing each character trait

The things that I'd been looking for and wanting had been written down
And line by line and word for word, I knew what I had found

Not once had I listed good looks or a physical performance profound
There were no words requesting a sculpted body, Denzel looks or someone model bound

And if I'm being honest with myself and true to my health and well-being itself
There is a barrier that I've put up

If there were or had been hopes for new love, I squashed them
When I felt a wave of passion, or unexpected smiles from a word, a wish, a well planted kiss
… I struck it down

I did it, I admit it
Because I'm mad
At the time and investment I put into another
Blinded by the quiet calm in the eye of our tornado of a relationship
I wanted to make a hit out of a miss
Searching and praying for the winds to mellow into an all encompassing bless
Imposing my will and dishonoring what was best, but I survived, it was merely a test

So as I question whether I'm ready
To move on or remain single
As I ponder what is or may be
If I'm ready to mix and mingle

I'll keep in touch with my heart
And know there is a link
A still soft knowing that keeps me going
Or slows me down simply to think

So I'll embrace the mixed feelings
That have put my heart on hold, I'll pause and wait
No pressure as I choose to work through
A lesson or two on how to truly appreciate a future mate

I Apologize

I'm sorry for your loss
The hopes and dreams you had
Of love for a lifetime and a
Wealth of experiences in a relationship that kept you glad

I'm sorry about the pain
That penetrated your heart
And the unexpected separation, the blind-sided division
That ripped your family apart

I'm sorry that your desires
Were not met as you would have had them to be
And the covenant that you were loyal to
Was not adhered to by, she

I'm sorry that your commitment
The one you were most serious about
Was not taken seriously
And your world was rocked
Shaken and did dismount

I pray that your days become lighter
And your hurt heals itself away
And the wound you suffered
Completely heals
And your wholeness returns
And you know the fullness of God blessing your days

Surrender

I am a better person
Because of you…

I am more aware~ I still love you, I will always care
Although it may not be expressed the same
My feelings have grown
I am forever changed

The time, the moments, the love we shared
Were a high, a joy, many dull moments spared

I'll always hope the best will come to you
As many of God's blessings
As you can stand your whole life through

I have no regret, nothing was done in vain
I will focus on the greatness
Of the love and life we exchanged

I will not say good-bye to you
I can't because you're still here
I won't forget how much you meant
The feelings are still very clear

The changes
Oh the changes will take some getting used to
But I sincerely wish, if we can both handle it
That we remain dear friends
Who can shoot the breeze, send up prayers for
Support one another's dreams
Share some laughter and yes a smile
I still thank God
For creating you and leading us to cross paths for a while

Just Who

Just who would I be
If I wasn't me
Exercising my choice to think…
About what lies in front of me
Or the steps I've gone past
Striking balance with my decisions
And a conscious that lasts

The path that I walk
A path that unwinds
Into whatever I choose…
Gracefully leading me to
The woman
I strive to
be
A warm,
loving soul
Who
thrives
Centered
in her
heart
Living a
joyful life
always and
forever,
peacefully

I Write Because I Must

I eat, sleep, pray, exercise and write
Oh yeah, I raise kids, teach, preach and work
Pay bills, clean house, dress up, look cute and flirt
I wake, often in the middle of the night
Reach for a pen and scribble some new insight
Sometimes with, other times without a light
I can tell the difference the next day as I attempt to read it
Recapping thoughts, theme, a mood or laughable whit

I search for words that are meaningful
Or full of meaning and make good sense
Lighten the atmosphere, make my shoulders less tense
Relaxing, not taxing
Bringing pleasure, memories to treasure
Jewels, gems of wisdom, reflection and thought
Expressing and sharing the intangible, *inspiration~* which can't be bought

I use a pen and paper, to express what comes from within
And in case your ears were plugged the first time I said it
Let me declare it again…
I (meaning me) write (mark or trace on a surface) because (which means~ for a reason) I (meaning me) must (am obliged)

Thank you for being part of my dream. I have wanted to write a book for as long as I can remember. I've heard people ask what I was waiting for and wondered- what I was waiting for. Well no one is waiting anymore! There are many times when I wake in the middle of the night or have ideas swirl in my mind throughout the day. Those ideas become strings of words that inspire me to write. Perhaps ideas come to you, targeted toward something you dream about doing or creating. Focus on those ideas, they have validity and purpose in your life… if you so choose. Imagine how different the world would be if Oprah Winfrey never began to speak up and out. Suppose Donald Trump never began investing his money or Maya Angelou never shared her story. Well, inside you is a seed that is growing, with the potential to flourish and spread as far and as wide as you're willing to go. Opportunity is all around you, no matter who you are or how things seem to be going. Believe it, see it and start opening doors and windows that will take you to the next step in discovering it! If this book has inspired you, shed any light or given you any helpful insight please communicate that with me. You can e-mail me at MiddleOfLove@hotmail.com. I'd love to hear any positive feedback that your heart leads you to share.

Love always,
Lisa

In the end... love always wins~

About the Author

Lisa Lipscomb is a mother, elementary school teacher, and poet. She has had a passion for writing 'forever.' Her skills were recognized at Development Centers, Inc. in Detroit, Michigan and she was given the job as Editor-in-Chief for the New Chance Times, a publication created for the teen parent program. **Somewhere in the Middle of Love** is her first book… there will be more to come.